the sun is kind to you

blln

ISBN: 979-8-218-84562-9

2nd Edition, 2025

contents

the sun is kind to you

the sun is kind to you

the sun is kind to
you
it burns you
just enough to
bring your beauty to
the surface
and when I shield
my eyes
from it in the
morning
or the
evening
I think about your short
breaths
the way
you gave into
me
for a little while
how we
thought we
finally found

what we'd been
doing so poorly
without
our
heartstrings tied
in
foolish knots
our light
misleading
in the dark

and I dreamt of you

and I dreamt of you
clumsy and eager
in your ways

full of passion,
wild
and
resolute

an honest
willing spirit

tender with
purpose

like
a
flower

blooming

an education

as the years stack up
I find the answers
to my oldest
questions
in strange places

I find philosophy
in a cup of coffee

I find love in a gesture

I find faith
in aimless stories
and
unsure smiles

I've been built,
rebuilt,
and will
build
again

a bubble

you are like
a bubble
climbing
and falling
with miraculous
sensitivity
and strength
always happening
to hit the
light
at just the
right angles
revealing
and
illuminating
what appears to be magic

I think you could break my heart

I barely know you
but I think you
could break my heart

your brain and
body
and your movements
and your voice

unlock something
strange
in me

I barely know you
but I think
the way you were
put together
fits with how I was put together

and I think you could
break
my heart

language

I'm out
of
words

I've just
got a
feeling

I don't think
it's possible to
write it

I've never read it

but
you carry it
somehow

a feast

there is a
tremendous
feast—

a neighborhood
of second chances
and
an industry of kindness.

there are evenings
in thick
primary
colors,

evenings
with
unexpected
fingertips on your
arm

and
jets making
slow
short dashes
in the sky

satisfied

you sit cross-legged.
on my bed,
a stripe of sun
across your lap,
bending the day
to
your will,

and you're cruel
with your beauty,
the stamp of approval
that nature
has planted
like an eager
kiss,
you abuse it
and the love
that others
slay dragons
for,

what
lands softly in your
hands

days

I wanted to get my
thoughts down
about you
quickly

but
it's been
days
already

stale
and
useless
days

days
overrun
with the
common

underwhelmed

and
abused

days
melted
by
indecision

and
indifferent
heat

days
and
days

without
you
around

it's good

it's odd to find someone
without having to look

someone
where words
aren't necessary,
where
being there is all you really need
and when they're not there
they are there
somehow

and it's
good

who wouldn't love you?

you're out of reach
and on my mind,
you're self-conscious
but feel the need to speak
and you do
in your small voice,
saying nothing special
but still smiling
letting
beauty spill
out
onto your skin
from the wells
inside you
and
you have perfect posture
and you tug at your ponytail
making sure it touches your
back just
right,

and who wouldn't love you,
who gets to touch you
and
why aren't there fingerprints?

she's trained the birds

she's trained the birds
to rise with
the sun,

given them reason
to sing
and
meter to their song,

she's in the
scent of
coffee,

at least in
my coffee,

that I brew in
no special
way

are you a joke

when I wake up
and think of your
small sneakers on
the sidewalk
and
when
the blinds do their best
to hold
the
morning back

and I brush my teeth and
think of
your thighs on
the passenger seat,
your teeth on my
neck,

your heart
on your sleeve

off your doorstep
and into the street

the night doesn't die
and the
day doesn't die
they just
switch places
for a while
and
when the sun is hiding
behind your
apartment
building
and
after
they ring the last
church bell,
before they go in
to meditate and pray
and do the laundry

there is something
that hangs in the
air,
a holy thing
that slides between
the midnight cars
and unloads the loneliest kisses
onto the loneliest
people

it's moving

I hear the heaters come on,
I hear the water pipes
and I hear the footsteps

I feel the time moving
I feel it leaving;
I wrestle with the
morning
and
you
are a dolphin
in the waves

I wonder about your breath

I wonder about your breath
and how our noses would
fit
and
I wonder if you'd stare
out the window while
I drove
or
if you watch
tv laying flat
on your back
with your knees in the air

I wonder if your voice
sounds the same way
to other people
and
if your laugh
echoes a little bit for
them too.

I wonder about your breath,
how it stands in cold air
or in my ear
but mostly, before
a kiss

my dreams of you

my dreams of you
drop like ink into
water,
blossoming
and
twisting
into shapes beyond
reason,
failing and creating
on the edge of
brilliance
until finally
the water
grays

paperback heart

I have a paperback
heart
dog-eared and creased
by the world,

the colors
are faded
and the spine is worn
but I'm glad
to see
it's finally in
good
hands

standing next to you

the vicious hymns
beams
and
easy melodies you
bring

slow down time

the bells

I don't think I was ever as amused
with music
as she was

the way the
hammers fell on
piano strings
or the way
breath made its
way
through any brass
instrument

I don't know if I got it
like she got it
because she would suddenly get
silent
when the bells rang
through
the glass of our window

as we didn't do much on a
sunday morning

I like you

you can build love like
music and fire,

explain the shape
of falling water,

you can
watch the
dust strain through sunlight

and in the morning
when the night melts off

and in the morning
when the
night melts off
and you
run
the shower
and I leave
to do
the things I need
to do

I start the car
and the song that
was cut short
with the engine
the night before
comes to life
again
but it
has no more power,

it is
a cartoon,
it is thin,
it is worthless

and I head
out into the pink
light,

I switch the turn
signal on
and
do my best to
wait

you do your best

it's happened to everyone
and it will happen again

it's why people
play the accordion
or
stare at the red numbers
of the bedside clock

and
you can't really fix it,
it stays with you

but it makes you better

because
when you step up to
the plate the next time
you'll be smarter
and
quicker

you'll know
the right angles
and instincts,

you'll know
when to give
and what to give
and how to take

you'll be
a genius,

the master
of
your heart

somewhere after something

she threw something
into the pacific ocean,
I couldn't quite tell
what it was,
maybe it was
a bottle,
maybe a
cup,

I think it had some
significance to her,
the act of throwing it,
not the item,
it bobbed out there in the
waves
and I could sense that
she had expected it to
sink.

we were strangers and we were at
the edge of the world,

there were birds there too,
they were odd,
black and like rubber,
and without warning they
would
twist and dive down,
deep
somewhere
after
something

your voice helped

your voice
helped,
I was down
and out,
way out,
and your voice
hit the
notes that
they struggle
for
in
symphonies—
how did I manage to
wring you out of this
life?

what you do

I don't know what
you're trying to
do

and if you
even know how to
do it

but you've made yourself
known to
me
in a very
impressive way

you've shaken
what I thought was
sturdy

and
you've made your
own path
in a place that
was overgrown

you've done
acrobatics
and poetry

you've changed the
morning and the
mountains

you've done what
you
do

and you did
it
well

let's

let's
take the fire exit out
of our pale lives,
break bread with
thorough losers,
rain dance in the
mojave,
waste
springtime
in alaska,
wander like satellites
under full moons
investing
in nothing
and
getting
it all
back

let's
swing hard
and miss,
gamble our soles
on uneven ground,
travel like
fire ants,
crazy,

led by something
we
can't
see

if you do not want me

if you do not want
me

I will live a monk's
life,
not become a monk
but
live in that fashion,
wake up
and
live for the
act of existing
and not for
success or
gain

I will forsake
ambition and
try my best to
slide in with the
birds
and
lions,

those that
follow the invisible
trail of spirit and
science
and use their hearts to
move only blood

and I'm sure that
sometimes I will
fail in this

that
I will meet
some mornings
with sleepless eyes

and
feel the exact
pain
of knowing that
you chose another
over me
and
that he feels your touch
and knows the curve of your
neck

and the small changes in your voice
as you
find the right words
to
express what's
swimming in your
head

I will work myself
to exhaustion
to keep
the desire away

and I will wrestle with
my dreams
to keep your
face from behind
my eyes

I will
turn myself over
to the elements,
to the day,
to the endless,
mindless, and
holy
rhythm

if you do not
want
me.

everyone's in love with you

everyone's in love with you
so I pretend I'm not

I know that if I
climb into
the competition for
your arms
that
I will slip through

that I will
become another face
in a fawning
crowd

another promise
in a feast of promises

so
I have stretched
and strangled
my heart
into
shapes
that
cannot hold
you

so that one day
I may hold you
myself

a solution

it was cold
so we built a fire

it was silent
so we brought guitars

it was sad
so we laughed

and as the sun went down
it came through your hair
like stained glass

knots

there are accidental
knots
made between people

knots boats
and
shoelaces can't use

knots that make
near strangers
spoonfeed you soft-serve ice cream
and
get them glasses of water
in the middle of the night

knots that are so
complicated
that you can never
really get them all the way
out

I tried to write you a letter

I've seen you
worn out,
at the end
on your belly,
beaten
by
a wicked world,
cheated
by a
trivial life
that has no
time for
kind words
and thoughtful
pauses,
but
if you can stay
the way you are
for just a little while
longer

your enemies
will fail,

the darkness
will fail
in your
light,
and you
will not
ever
be
moved

I saw you

I saw you
you looked good

like you're finally becoming the
person you were meant to be

like
you have found a
balance between
how to give the
world what it needs

and how to
hold on
to what you
need.

I saw you

farther from the
edge

and

you looked good.